THE
BRIDGES YURI BUILT

Written by
Kai Naima Williams

Illustrated by
Anastasia M. Williams

KAEPERNICK
PUBLISHING

DEDICATIONS

Kai Naima Williams

Writing this book was a true passion project, one that was made possible by the tremendous support of my communities. Thank you to Noah Ballard and Verve Agency, my Dream Team of collaborators: Christopher Petrella, Tony Ng, Traci N. Todd, Anastasia Magliore Williams, and to Colin Kaepernick for giving me the platform to share Yuri's story. Thank you to Michael Arndt, Simone Roberts-Payne, Zurich Deleon, Grandma Audee, Akemi, the whole Kochiyama fam, and, of course, Mom and Dad for all your guidance and encouragement.

Anastasia M. Williams

For my grandparents, who built bridges with their backs, and carried us all forward and upward.

www.KaepernickPublishing.com

Printed in Canada with union labor.

Editorial: Traci N. Todd & Christopher Petrella • Art Direction: Tony Ng • Project Management: Christopher Petrella & Kerem Ozguz

Distributed by Two Rivers Distribution

ISBN: 978-1-960571-00-7

THE
BRIDGES
YURI BUILT

Written by
Kai Naima
Williams

Illustrated by
Anastasia M.
Williams

KAEPERNICK
PUBLISHING

Yuri Kochiyama was born Mary Yuriko Nakahara on May 19, 1921 in San Pedro, California. She was Nisei, which meant that her parents came from Japan, but she and her brothers were born in the United States. Even though the Nakaharas were one of the few Japanese American families in town, Yuri always felt like she belonged in San Pedro.

Yuri loved the sweet things in life: poetry, hymns, hikes and bike rides by the sea, baseball games, and what the Bible said about compassion and treating others with kindness. More than anything, Yuri loved people. She reported for the local paper, volunteered with the Girl Scouts, and taught Sunday school. Any club or crew she could join, Yuri was eager to count herself a member.

One dark December day in 1941, Big News boomed from the radio:
Japanese planes had bombed Pearl Harbor, in Hawaii! It wasn't long before
two men in black suits stood at her door. "Can I help you?" Yuri asked.

Like two great gusts of wind, the men rushed past her, whirling around the house knocking over books and plants. They grabbed her father and ushered him out the door. "Wait!" Yuri shouted, but just like wind, the men disappeared as swiftly as they'd come.

That night, Yuri's mother cried until her eyes had no tears left to give.
The men were government agents. They had taken her father in for questioning.
They believed he was a spy, just because he was Japanese.

"But we're American too!" Yuri exclaimed.

Weeks later, Yuri's father was released. He was so frail and sick that he seemed to waver on the border of life and the beyond. Yuri looked in his eyes and saw a ghostly man who did not recognize her. By the next day, he was gone.

His death plunged her into startling sorrow. Lost in her grief, Yuri didn't notice the world around her beginning to change.

After Pearl Harbor, the United States declared war on Japan. Suddenly, the neighbors turned their backs on Yuri and her family. They glared at them in the street, or walked right past them without a glance or greeting. For the first time, she felt like an outsider in her own town.

By the winter, all Japanese American people were forced to board trains heading far, far away to concentration camps that would hold them for the remainder of the war. The Nakaharas were taken to the Santa Anita Race Track, where they would have to live before being assigned to a camp. Their tiny room stank of horses and hay and held only a cot and one dingy light hanging from the ceiling.

After several months, the Nakaharas were transferred to a camp in Jerome, Arkansas, 1,800 miles away from their home in San Pedro. The camps were a wasteland with block housing, ringed with barbed wire fences and dotted with watchtowers where guards oversaw the imprisoned people. In summer, the humid heat made them sweat and stick to their clothes, but winters were worse. With only a potbelly stove in each barrack to keep them warm, the people struggled not to freeze. All year, the Jerome rainfall turned the ground swampy with mud.

It isn't fair, Yuri thought. *If America is really the land of the free, how can we be treated like prisoners in our own country?*

Still, people built furniture out of driftwood and sewed curtains and bedspreads to brighten up the barracks. They planned activities and planted flowers. They did everything they could to make the camps feel a little more like home.

Yuri had never met so many other Japanese people. They came from parts of California and the islands of Hawaii, from farms and fishing towns. In the mess halls, they told her their stories over dinner. They taught her about Japanese culture and had long conversations about what it meant to be Japanese in America. Many young Nisei men had chosen to join the U.S. Army, eager to prove their loyalty to their country. But lots of people at the camps were angry with the government, and Yuri was starting to understand why.

When the Nisei soldiers came to visit the camp, Yuri was the first to greet them. "What's your name? Where are you from?" She asked, bursting with questions.

A handsome soldier stepped forward and answered: "I'm Bill Kochiyama," he said, with a glint in his eye. "I come from Manhattan Island." What island is that? Yuri wanted to know. Bill hoped to show her some day. At the camp party, they danced the night away. After he left Jerome to return to boot camp, Yuri wrote to Bill every week. Then once, twice, three times a day.

Before long, their messages became love letters, and Bill asked Yuri to marry him.

In a letter, Bill told her, "I feel so lucky to have someone to write and talk to all the time. All the Nisei boys here feel lonely and the other soldiers stay away from us. They hardly get any letters at all."

Yuri hated to think of all those brave young men missing their homes and families and friends. *What could she do to help them?* She wondered.

Then Yuri had a big idea: What if she wrote letters to all the Nisei soldiers so they wouldn't feel alone? But she couldn't do it by herself. Yuri gathered up her Sunday school class and told them her plan.

They called themselves the Crusaders. They sent letters with candy, little songs, and daily doodles. They told the soldiers tales about life at camp and the friends they had made. Mostly, they wrote how proud they were of them.

When the boys wrote back, they thanked their new pen pals over and over. The letters made them feel loved.

Soon, the Crusaders' letter-writing campaign spread to other camps. They reached more than three thousand soldiers in all.

When the war was over and the camps were closed, Yuri packed her bags and boarded a train to New York City, Bill's hometown, to start their new life.

Finding work in New York was not easy. She looked for a job as a waitress, but all the restaurants turned her away. "We don't hire Japs," they said as they slammed doors in her face.

Finally, she got a job in a coffee shop downtown. The dishwashers and cooks were Black men and women. They told her about their lives. About the hardships and hate and how they were barred from living in certain neighborhoods, working certain jobs, or eating in restaurants reserved for white people only.

Yuri felt anger bubble like lava inside her chest. She wanted to knock down the country and build it back up into a place where everybody was free and treated fairly.

Yuri and Bill got a little place in Harlem, hardly bigger than a train car!
Together, they made a family.

Harlem was a new world. The center of Black culture in New York.

Yuri and Bill joined the Harlem Parents' Committee, a group that was fighting for safer streets and better schools in the neighborhood. At one protest, mothers and fathers sat with their babies in the road. They held tight to one another, stopping the flow of cars and shutting down the busy street.

How powerful it was, to know that together, the crowd of protesters could not be broken through. Suddenly, Yuri knew: This was the work she was meant to do.

"IF THE MOVEMENT WILL HAVE ME, I MUST DO EVERYTHING IN MY POWER TO HELP."

She knew Black people were working to fight against racist laws in New York and all across the country. The fight was called the Civil Rights Movement, and Yuri longed to join. But would she be accepted?

She remembered the war and how people treated her as a suspect, an outsider, because she wasn't one of them.

But she remembered the camps as well. Even though she wasn't Black, she knew how it felt to be denied freedom because of the color of her skin.

If the movement will have me, I must do everything in my power to help, she decided. But how to begin?

Yuri started just by showing up. Every meeting, every action, every protest, she was present.

She took notes and made signs, she passed out petitions and dropped flyers around town. She joined a Freedom School and studied the writings and speeches of leaders like Fannie Lou Hamer, Marcus Garvey, and Malcolm X.

Her journals overflowed with pages of news from the front lines of the movement: the marches in Mississippi, the sit-ins in Georgia, and the names of all the many activists who'd been jailed in Alabama.

People started to wonder, who was this little Asian lady who sat in the back of every meeting? But the more she showed up, the more they invited her in.

Soon everyone in Harlem knew, if you needed a place to stay, just write to Yuri, and she'd give you food and shelter. People came in droves: orphans and runaways, tourists and New Yorkers, journalists from Japan, musicians from Hawaii, and freedom fighters from every corner of the South.

When all beds were full, Bill slept in the bathtub and Yuri crawled into the crib with the baby.

Every Saturday night they threw an Open House. Neighbors and strangers, artists and activists came. They played the ukulele, they danced the hula, they sang. They read speeches and spoke of action and change. From sundown to dawn, the party raged on.

No matter who arrived, everyone was made to feel they belonged. Folks called the apartment Grand Central Station, for the thousands of people who passed through. And one day, Malcolm X, the great freedom fighter, came to visit.

Yuri and Bill were hosting a group of visitors from Japan, victims who had survived the Hiroshima bombings during World War II. Malcolm came to meet them, and the whole neighborhood showed up to greet him. In Yuri's crowded living room, he stood tall and loomed large. And when he spoke, the room fell hushed.

"EDUCATION IS THE PASSPORT TO THE FUTURE... ...FOR TOMORROW BELONGS TO THE PEOPLE WHO PREPARE FOR IT TODAY."

He told them about parts of the world where Black and Brown people lived under the control of white, western nations, places where people suffered racism and poverty.

He shared what he had learned of the histories of Africa and Asia and what they had in common. He urged them to protest America's new war in Vietnam, and told them that the struggle of the Vietnamese people was the same struggle of people of color all over the world.

Soon after, Malcolm left for a long trip to a place called Mecca. As he traveled, he sent postcards to Yuri with stories about movements and uprisings in many countries. "The people here," he wrote, "are fast leaping out of the past into the future!"

Yuri treated each postcard like a precious treasure, and over the months her collection grew. As Malcolm wrote to her, she wrote to others too.

Yuri learned of activists all over the world imprisoned by their own governments—and the governments of other countries—for speaking out. In the movement, they called these activists political prisoners. Since powerful forces wanted to keep the activists far away from their communities, they had little hope of going home.

So she began to write them letters. She sent letters with money and books. Letters with news from the movement to remind them that every day, on the outside, people were working to free them. Through many long nights, she stayed up at her kitchen table writing, writing, writing.

In the prisons, the name Yuri Kochiyama spread like wildfire. Everyone knew: Yuri was the first person you called when you got in, and the first person you called when you got out. "I am always here for you," she promised.

When Malcolm came back from Mecca, Yuri rejoiced. She couldn't wait to hear all he had learned from his travels and his new plans for the movement.

On February 21, 1965, less than a year after his return, she sat in the front row of the Audubon Ballroom in Harlem anxiously awaiting his speech. But just as Malcolm stepped up to the stage, Yuri heard several loud BANGS! For a moment the room was silent and still. Then people started to scream. They ran for the exits. Yuri ran to the stage.

She
cradled Malcolm's
head in her lap.

She

cried his name

over and over.

But

Malcolm

was gone.

That night no one, not even Bill, could soothe Yuri's grief.
What's the point of trying to change this world? she thought. *There is too much hate keeping us apart!*

She looked out of her window at the long stretch of Harlem streets, and the midnight sky above. While her spirit felt as blue and dark as that sky, something inside her still ached for light.

Then Yuri remembered Malcolm's visit, the words he had spoken in the very spot where she sat.

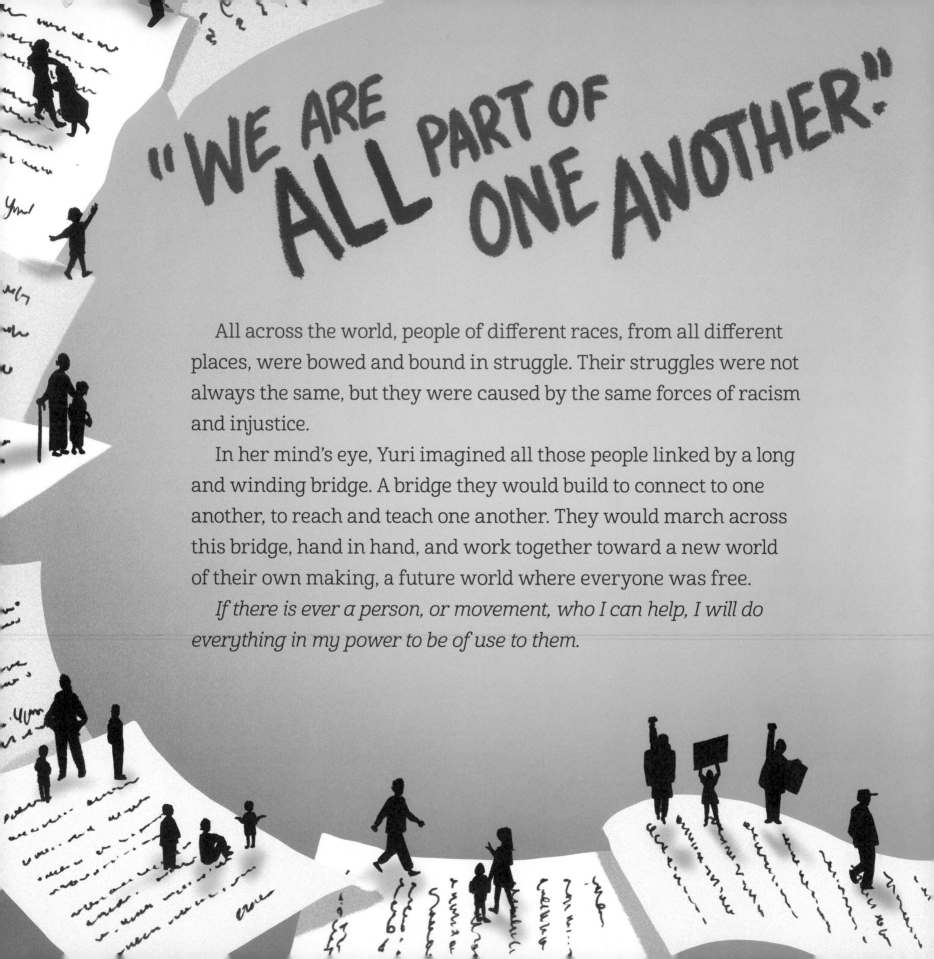

"WE ARE ALL PART OF ONE ANOTHER."

All across the world, people of different races, from all different places, were bowed and bound in struggle. Their struggles were not always the same, but they were caused by the same forces of racism and injustice.

In her mind's eye, Yuri imagined all those people linked by a long and winding bridge. A bridge they would build to connect to one another, to reach and teach one another. They would march across this bridge, hand in hand, and work together toward a new world of their own making, a future world where everyone was free.

If there is ever a person, or movement, who I can help, I will do everything in my power to be of use to them.

From that night forth, Yuri leapt into her work as a freedom fighter, giving shelter, joining protests, making speeches, and lending her voice, her writings, her networks to the many people, from many movements, who sought her aid.

With every step, every person she met, every letter she sent, she kept on building her bridge.

Growing up in the Kochiyama family, I often had the sense that my great-grandmother was known and loved by many, but I didn't fully appreciate the extent of her activism, or her significance as a figure, until she passed away. In fact, it was at her memorial service in Harlem that I can first recall realizing the breadth of her impact. When Angela Davis took the stage to pay tribute, she called Yuri "the person who can really change the world." Those words sparked a deep curiosity that continues to live within me to this day.

YURI KOCHIYAMA

I wanted to know why she was that person. What made Grandma Yuri so special?

As an organizer, Yuri is distinguished for her activism and her personality. She was a committed storekeeper of information and an avid documentarian who photographed every action, kept records of every person she met, and preserved every piece of correspondence over decades of work. She is also known for the scope and depth of her beliefs, namely, her commitment to seeking revolution. To have undergone such a dramatic transformation — from her patriotic and politically ambivalent upbringing to her radical antiracist, anti-imperialist ideology in adulthood—indicated that she was a true believer in the causes she supported and that her consciousness was constantly evolving with new understanding. She was steadfast in her values but open to change within her own beliefs. And most notably, she was invested in the pursuit of liberation for all oppressed peoples, and her advocacy was never limited to challenging the racism she experienced as an Asian American woman but extended to all kinds of communities. For Yuri, solidarity was not an ideal but an embodied, necessary practice.

Throughout her life, Yuri supported many movements. She was affiliated with the Black Panther Party, the Young Lords, the Republic of New Africa, the Student

> "Making connections between movements and identifying common sources of oppression remained a crucial component of her work until the end of her life."

Nonviolent Coordinating Committee, the Congress of Racial Equality, among countless other organizations. She personally supported and advocated on behalf of political prisoners, including Mtayari Shabaka Sundiata, Yu Kikumura, Marilyn Buck, Lolita Lebrón, Leonard Peltier, and Assata Shakur. Her activism took her across the country and the world, from riding in a U-Haul truck to Mississippi with citizens of the Republic of New Africa in 1971 to participating in the 1977 takeover of the Statue of Liberty with Puerto Rican Independentistas to demand the release of prisoner Andre Cordero, to traveling to Cuba with the Venceremos Brigade in 1987, to visiting Peru, Japan, and the Philippines in the early 1990s on human rights missions.

She was a critical advisor in the Asian American movement and, alongside her husband Bill, helped to organize for reparations for the incarceration of Japanese Americans during World War II. When President Ronald Reagan signed the Civil Liberties Act in 1988, which granted $20,000 to each Japanese American internment survivor, Yuri cited the act to advocate for reparations for African American descendants of enslaved people. And she continued to reference Japanese American experiences during WWII when speaking out against racial profiling toward Muslims, South Asians, and Middle Easterners in the United States post-9/11. Making connections between movements and identifying common sources of oppression remained a crucial component of her work until the end of her life.

When I meet people who knew Yuri, and even those who only encountered her once, I am struck by how often they repeat the same sentiments. They tell me she made them feel heard and cared for, that she always remembered them, that she received them with kindness, respect, and genuine interest. Yuri's ability to personally connect with people from all walks of life and to bring communities together, despite differences, to achieve common goals is part of what makes her such a beloved and unique figure. Those connections are the bridges Yuri built, and the legacy that she leaves behind.